Original title:
Songs of a Silver Winter

Copyright © 2024 Creative Arts Management OÜ
All rights reserved.

Author: Christian Leclair
ISBN HARDBACK: 978-9916-94-540-7
ISBN PAPERBACK: 978-9916-94-541-4

Whispers of Frosted Dreams

In a flurry, snowflakes dance,
They tickle noses, take a chance.
Frosty breath forms little clouds,
While squirrels giggle in their shrouds.

Hot cocoa spills, a marshmallow fight,
Slipping on ice, a comic sight.
Laughter echoes, joy will gleam,
Under the moon, we chase a dream.

Melodies Beneath the Icicles

Icicles hang, sharp as a knife,
Hanging like laughter, full of life.
Snowmen wear hats that are too big,
As kids all around do a silly jig.

Snowball fights, the best of times,
Everyone sings, making rhymes.
Frosted trees with lights aglow,
Winter's humor, always on show.

Chiming Through the Snowfall

Jingle bells ring, but not quite right,
The dog joins in, what a silly sight!
Cramming in mittens, two left, one right,
We trip on our laughter, pure delight.

Finding a snowdrift, diving deep,
Gathering snow, a mountain heap.
A snow angel made, wings too wide,
In the winter's waltz, joy can't hide.

Echoes of the Winter Night

Under the moon, we glide and slide,
Stumbling softly, winter's ride.
Voices echo in the chilly air,
As we invent games, no moment spare.

Chattering teeth in playful glee,
A snowman wears my best old tee!
Giggles fly as snowflakes twirl,
In the frosty night, laughter unfurl.

Rhapsody in White Silence

The snowflakes fall like tiny stars,
With snowmen posing, looking bizarre.
A penguin glides on frozen ground,
While children laugh in joy profound.

Hot cocoa spills on mittens warm,
As winter winds begin to charm.
The sleds go flying, thud and crash,
And in the air, a snowball splash!

Frosted Embrace of Twilight

Icicles dangle from rooftops high,
While squirrels wear coats that might defy.
The moon peeks out, a silver grin,
And frosty cheeks are sure to win.

Wind chimes tinkle, singing tunes,
As snowflakes dance 'neath dreaming moons.
Hot soup spills on the kitchen floor,
As laughter echoes, we all want more!

Melancholy of the Winter Skies

Clouds gather round like a fuzzy quilt,
While temperatures dip, so cozy, no guilt.
The snowman sighs, a floppy hat,
And penguins waddle like this and that.

Cupcakes freeze in the cooling air,
While ice slips under feet unaware.
We wrap up tight, all snug and warm,
In winter's grip, a quirky charm!

A Dance on the Icebound Lake

Skaters spin with laughter bright,
As ice is smooth, a joyful sight.
The ducks wear scarves, oh what a flair,
While twirls and falls fill up the air.

Frosty noses, a rosy hue,
As tipsy moves make giggles ensue.
Yet someone slips and takes a dive,
And all burst into laughter, oh so alive!

Sorrow and Beauty in the Cold

Snowflakes dance with glee,
While penguins sip their tea.
A snowman lost his hat,
Said, "Where's my frosty cat?"

Icicles hang like teeth,
From every roof beneath.
The cold wind gives a shout,
"Who said winter's all about?"

Tales in the Whispering Snow

Once a squirrel named Lou,
Wore boots that were too blue.
He slipped on icy floors,
And landed on all fours!

A rabbit wrote a book,
About the best snow nook.
In winter's frosty tale,
He claims he found a whale!

Chill of the Silver-Tipped Dawn

The early sun peeks in,
And shivers with a grin.
Frosty breath in the air,
Says, "Don't forget your chair!"

The trees all wear a cape,
A snowman starts to scrape.
He shouts, "I need a drink!"
But then he starts to sink!

Soundtrack of the Frosty Wanderer

A frosty wanderer laughed,
As he slipped on a daft.
His hat flew to a deer,
Who thought it was a spear!

They danced in snowy rings,
While the snowflakes played strings.
But then they lost the beat,
And fell right on their feet!

Frost-kissed Echoes

Snowflakes dance like bees in flight,
As we chase our hats in the fading light.
Hot cocoa spills, a frothy delight,
While squirrels plot their takeover of the night.

Icicles hang like daggers of doom,
Yet we laugh as we trip on the broom.
The chill wraps us like a fuzzy cocoon,
Turning our breath into a winter's tune.

Symphonies of the Icy Veil

The carolers sing, holding mugs in tow,
But one hits a high note, and off they go.
Snowmen grumble 'bout hats, feeling low,
While mittens rejoice in their match-making show.

A snowball fight turns cheery and wild,
With each splash of snow, laughter is piled.
The mailbox gets pelted, like a disgruntled child,
But even the mailman can't help but smile.

Solstice Serenades

Winter solstice, the sun takes a nap,
Yet we wear our warm sweaters, a jazzy mishap.
Cookies vanish, they make quite the trap,
While reindeer play hide and seek on the map.

The fire crackles, a popsicle's dream,
While cousins argue over board game schemes.
The dog joins the fray, plotting extreme,
Chewing on packages, he reigns supreme.

Nocturne Beneath the Starlit Drift

Starry nights twinkle, like lights on a tree,
While we stumble outside, clad in wild glee.
The frost bites our noses, we shout 'Whoopee!',
Engaging in snowball diplomacy.

Under the glow of the moon, we prance,
Tiptoeing on ice, what a comical dance!
Winter very well knows how to enhance,
Our clumsy attempts to give joy a chance.

Murmurs of Icy Reverie

The snowflakes giggle as they fall,
Dancing on rooftops, a winter ball.
Socks on my hands, a lost pair kicks,
In this frigid game, it's bricks and sticks.

Frosty breath shapes a silly face,
Wishing for hot chocolate, just in case.
Yet here I trudge, my scarf untied,
A frozen fashion faux pas, oh what a ride!

Whispered Wishes in the Snow

Snowmen grinning with carrot noses,
While snowball fights break out in poses.
One throws a ball, it's pure delight,
Oh dear, I'm pelted, what a sight!

Icicles hanging like frozen spears,
Daring the brave to face their fears.
Hot cocoa spills - I slip and slide,
With giggles echoing, I can't hide!

Radiance of the Frosted Moon

The night is bright, the moon's a prankster,
Chasing shadows, it gleams like a gangster.
Whispers of ice, a silly sight,
Snowflakes twirl, dancing in the light.

Boots squeak and slip with every step,
Snowballs ready, it's time to prep.
A snow angel made - oh what a flair,
Only to find that I'm stuck in there!

Nightingale's Chill Serenade

Birds cheerfully chirp through the chill,
While I chase snowflakes, I stumble, I thrill.
Slipping on ice, I reach for a tree,
A rather grand tumble - there goes my tea!

In winter's grasp, we laugh and play,
Adventures in snow, brightening the day.
Frost kisses noses, cheeks rosy red,
Nightingales sing as we laugh instead!

A Dance Beneath the Silver Sky

In a world of ice where penguins glide,
Santa's lost his sleigh, took a joyride.
Snowmen wearing shades, dance with flair,
While snowflakes giggle, twirling in the air.

Hot cocoa's spilling, marshmallows fly,
The reindeer are laughing, oh my, oh my!
A polar bear juggles, quite a show,
As kids chase their shadows, to and fro.

Frosty footprints lead to a pie,
Baked in the oven, oh me, oh my!
The gingerbread men are on parade,
Waving their icing, unafraid!

At twilight's dance, the stars awake,
With a wink and a smile, they're all at stake.
In this silver wonder, so light and free,
Laughter erupts in sweet jubilee.

Enchanted Frost and Gentle Thoughts

A squirrel in mittens collects acorns today,
While snowflakes chime in their glistening ballet.
A toasty fire crackles, tales are spun,
Of a snowman who thought he could run!

With snowballs launched, there's giggles and squeals,
As everyone tumbles in frosty wheel deals.
The moon dips low, all covered in fluff,
While hot chocolate mugged, says, "That's enough!"

Elves in their workshop, crafting some glee,
Wrapped up in mischief, as happy as can be.
With candy canes swinging, their laughter flows,
In this wonderland where anything goes!

As night takes a bow, and stars wink bright,
In this chilly charm, everything feels right.
So dance through the frost, with smiles at play,
And chase the cold worries all away!

Shadows and Snowflakes' Embrace

In the still of the night, shadows take flight,
While snowflakes whisper, gleaming so bright.
A cat on a roof wears a snow-white cap,
While dreaming of mice in a cozy nap.

The snow shovels out a chore so grand,
But watch out for slip-ups in the land!
A ginger cat grumbles, not wanting to go,
While snowmen crack jokes, throwing snow.

With each flake that falls, a giggle's in place,
As the breeze nudges hats off at a rapid pace.
Children in mittens tumble and spin,
While polar bears cuddle, wearing a grin.

A starry-eyed owl, perched high in a tree,
Winks with amusement at the joyful spree.
The world may be chilly, but hearts shine bright,
In this wintry wonder, all feels just right.

Stories of the Glacial Silence

In the hush of the snow, secrets unfold,
Where icicles dangle, like silver and gold.
A flurry of penguins plays peek-a-boo,
While polar bears slide, wishing for two!

Snowflakes flutter down, each unique in design,
As frosty whispers giggle, with every shine.
The frost sprites are plotting a mischievous scheme,
To steal all the hot cups of cocoa, it seems!

As icicles glitter, like chandeliers bright,
A blizzard of laughter bursts into the night.
With wrapped fuzzy blankets, and jokes oh so merry,
The cold may be bitter, but hearts are quite cheery!

So gather your friends, for a warm winter tale,
With shivers and giggles, we'll never derail.
In this frosty playground, where dreams come alive,
Laughter's the secret that helps us survive!

Serene Chimes from Frozen Pines

In the woods, trees wear hats,
Dressed in snow, they look like cats.
A squirrel slips on icy ground,
While whispers laugh, without a sound.

Chirps from birds, all fluffed and neat,
Wobbling on their frosty feet.
Hot cocoa spills, a funny sight,
Who knew winter could be so light?

Icicles dangle, honest fate,
A glistening feast, we just can't rate.
Frosty pants on kids abound,
While winter fun is lost, not found.

But cheer is here, beneath the gray,
As snowmen dance in bright ballet.
Winter's chill can't steal our glee,
In this frosted jubilee!

Hushed Verses of the Silver Boughs

Under trees with branches bare,
Penguins laugh beyond compare.
Bundled tight, we waddle past,
Making snowballs, oh so fast.

Twirling scarves, all red and bright,
Tiptoeing through the frosty night.
A snowflake lands upon my nose,
Giggles follow wherever it goes.

Hot soup waits at the cabin's door,
While frosty fingers beg for more.
Slippery paths lead to great retreats,
As laughter echoes in quick beats.

Mittens fly across the ground,
In this winter, joy is found.
Even when the cold feels strong,
We make the silly moments long!

Echoes of the Hazy Dusk

A snowman wears a funny grin,
With buttons made from old tin spin.
His arms are sticks, his hat a cap,
As winter sing, we jump and clap.

The skies all gray, with twinkling light,
Chasing shadows, we laugh in fright.
Sudden slips on icy land,
Where every tumble is grand and planned.

Carols sung by frozen lips,
Skating fields bring joyful trips.
Twinkling lights in windows glow,
While winter fun puts on a show.

As frosty breezes tease the air,
We skip around without a care.
With every chill, a chuckle grows,
Our hearts are warm, as winter flows!

Chilled Whispers of the Heart

The snowflakes dance, a wild ballet,
While we all bundle up to play.
With every catch, a giggle bursts,
Fueled by cocoa and snowball thirsts.

Frosty noses, cheeks like red,
Laughter mingles, joy widespread.
Pine trees sing in muted bliss,
As every flake is pure and kissed.

Mittens tossed and sleds that fly,
Echoes of laughter fill the sky.
Falling into piles of white,
We rise again, what pure delight!

So let the chilly winds blow rough,
With warmth inside, our hearts stay tough.
Winter might be cold and stark,
But in our giggles, there's a spark!

Lullaby of the Shivering Stars

The stars are cold and snuggled tight,
They shiver and they shake at night.
Moonbeams dance on frosty roofs,
While snowflakes laugh and lose their poofs.

A penguin tries to skateboard fast,
He tumbles over, what a blast!
The night is filled with chirps and squeaks,
While squirrels sing their winter streaks.

The chilly breeze gets frosty feet,
And tickles noses, oh what a treat!
Hot cocoa spills on fluffy paws,
As critters giggle without a pause.

Sleepy stars in twinkling hats,
Join in the fun with purring cats.
They hum a rhyme, but all mistake,
For every laugh, they start to shake.

Ballads of the Glimmering Dawn

The morn arrives with winks and grins,
As coffee brews and laughter spins.
A snowman tries to do a jig,
With carrots flopping, oh so big!

Sunrise stretches, yawns, and beams,
While squirrels scheme in glittering dreams.
A gingerbread man starts to sway,
He's lost his gumdrop on the way.

Pancakes stack up, a towering sight,
With syrup rivers, oh what a height!
The toaster pops in gleeful cheer,
While butter jives, oh my, oh dear!

Snowflakes twirl like dancers bright,
As winter's chorus takes to flight.
Each giggle dances, pure delight,
In this frosty morning light.

Aria of the Winter Winds

The winter winds begin to sing,
They whistle tunes of frosty bling.
A snowflake spins upon the breeze,
While chipmunks aim their acorn peas.

A polar bear in shades so chic,
Tries telling jokes, they're all quite weak.
He slips on ice, does a ballet,
While penguins cheer and shout, 'Hooray!'

Frosty trails where snowmen race,
With carrot noses in the chase.
But wait! One tumbles, lands with a thud,
While icicles clap, 'Oh what a dud!'

The winds invite, a zany show,
With laughs and giggles in the snow.
They sing to stars that twinkle bright,
In a wild and wintry night.

Echoing Shadows on Snowy Paths

Footprints leave a trail of glee,
As shadows dance with whimsy spree.
A snowball fight erupts with cheer,
While giggling fills the frosty sphere.

A rabbit hops with such delight,
He's wearing boots, they're just too tight!
He stumbles, flips, a snowy twirl,
And lands right next to a dizzy pearl.

While trees stand tall in snowy hoods,
Raccoons juggle with their foods.
A squirrel tries to take a bow,
But rolls away, can't help but wow!

Echoes linger with jolly sounds,
As joy and laughter swirl around.
In winter's grip, we play and cheer,
With every shadow, warmth draws near.

Mystical Lyrics in the Snowfall

Beneath the snowflakes' playful tease,
A squirrel steals snacks with awkward ease.
Frosty whispers dance in the air,
As penguins in hats waddle without a care.

Icicles hang like frozen spoons,
They tinkle and jingle with silly tunes.
Snowmen wobble on carrot toes,
While winter fairies swap their glowing clothes.

A snowball fight breaks the chilly peace,
Laughter erupts, the worries cease.
The moon peeks in with a wink, so bright,
As snowflakes twirl in a silly flight.

There's magic found beneath the frost,
In giggles and grins, we count the cost.
Each snowy patch, a canvas to score,
For memories made in winter's encore.

A Tapestry of Winter's Chords

In winter wonder, the tavern sings,
With mugs held high, the laughter springs.
An owl, in glasses, reads the news,
While mice twirl in their tiny shoes.

The fireplace crackles, a warm embrace,
As marshmallows roast in a sticky race.
Jolly elves juggle candy canes,
As frosty breezes play silly games.

A flurry of laughter drifts through the room,
As snowflakes pirouette, dispelling gloom.
With every joke, the cold takes flight,
And winter's chill feels wildly bright.

So join the chorus, on this snowy night,
For joy is found in the frosted light.
Let's dance and sing until the dawn,
In a winter's tale that carries on.

Enchantment Wrapped in Frost

Hats made of snow and scarves that glow,
Wrap up the whimsy in winter's flow.
A penguin's slip—a comic slide,
As snowflakes giggle and swirl with pride.

Winter critters in a hop and dash,
Making snow angels in a frosty splash.
With every chill that bites our nose,
Comes a hearty laugh that brightly grows.

Chubby snowmen with buttons awry,
Greet us with grins and a winked eye.
While children throw fluff in joyous mirth,
Creating a racket, delighting the earth.

So let's be merry beneath the pale light,
For laughter's the warmth on a crisp, cold night.
With enchanted whimsies, here's the proof,
Winter's a giggle, our hearts in a roof.

Rhythms of a Subzero Realm

The penguins dance in funky shoes,
While polar bears sip frosty brews.
Snowflakes swirl in silly spree,
As ice chimes ring with glee.

Little rabbits hop and twirl,
In this frosty, joyful whirl.
Laughter echoes, crisp and bright,
In the chill of winter's night.

Squirrels skate on frozen lakes,
While frosty llamas munch on flakes.
A snowman grins with carrot nose,
As winter winks and lightly doze.

With every flake, a tickle found,
As giggles dance upon the ground.
The world's a stage, in icy sights,
Where winter plays its funny nights.

Carols in the Snow-Blanketed Woods

In the woods, a choir sings,
With all the joy that winter brings.
Squirrels croon off-key, they say,
While deer lead in a grand ballet.

Snowmen sway with frosty hats,
As owls spin tales of winter chats.
Foxes prance like furry kings,
In this realm where laughter springs.

A winter tale of silly socks,
With penguins chasing funny clocks.
The trees all giggle, branches sway,
In a snow globe that forgot to play.

As moonlight dances on the snow,
These frosty tunes begin to flow.
A rhythm made of chuckles light,
Echoes softly through the night.

A Tapestry of Frost and Light

Frosty paintings line the walls,
Made by mischief, winter calls.
Each flake a note in this grand song,
Where silly critters just belong.

The snowflakes giggle, set to flight,
As penguins waddle left and right.
A moose in boots begins to jig,
With laughter loud, it feels so big.

Icicles dangle, spears of fun,
While snowmen roll till day is done.
A frosted world, a playful sight,
In this tapestry of pure delight.

Amid the chill, all hearts ignite,
As the frosty air brings sheer delight.
In every glimmer, every bite,
A world of joy shines oh so bright.

Twilight Sonatas

As daylight wanes, the frost appears,
Filled with snowball fight cheers.
Twilight paints the skies up high,
While snowflakes dance, oh my, oh my!

A choir of critters sings along,
In a winterized, silly throng.
The moon laughs down, a gentle guide,
As critters come out for the fun slide.

Snowy trails made by furry paws,
Giggles burst in little jaws.
A waltz of winter, bright and bold,
With side-splitting tales, forever told.

Amidst the chill, the laughter roams,
In a land that feels like home.
Where the night sings sweet and low,
And winter's giggles continue to flow.

Nocturne of the Frostbitten Night

Cold air nips at my nose,
While squirrels wear tiny clothes,
Snowmen shiver in the glow,
As the frozen winds do blow.

Icicles hang like chandeliers,
Laughing at our winter fears,
Bunnies hop in woolly socks,
Stomping down on frozen blocks.

Frosty breath becomes a plume,
As we dance in nature's room,
Chasing shadows, losing track,
In this icy, silly wrack.

Beneath the stars, we all prance,
While frosty feet begin to dance,
Winter's charm is cheeky fun,
With giggles echoing 'til dawn.

Carols of the Silent Woods

The owls hoot out of tune,
As I waltz beneath the moon,
Snowflakes tickle on my chin,
I trip over where I've been.

Squirrels chatter, chubby-cheeked,
In winter coats, they look so Greek,
The trees, now dressed in white lace,
Are hiding secrets in their space.

With snowballs flying, laughter loud,
I stand out in this winter crowd,
Each tree a wardrobe of display,
As critters laugh and dance away.

With frosty noses, we explore,
Seeking treasures, winter's lore,
The silent woods may seem so spry,
In this chilly, funny why.

Rhapsody in White Silence

Under blankets made of snow,
The world is quiet, here we go,
Whispers float on frosted air,
As winter's breath ruffles my hair.

The rabbits bob and leap around,
In droves, they scamper on the ground,
While I attempt a snowball throw,
And land face-first in winter's glow.

Cocoa warms my chilly hands,
With marshmallows that dance like bands,
The snowflakes twirl into a fight,
As laughter breaks the frosty night.

Holding hands, we spin like tops,
Slipping down the snowy drops,
In this quiet, giggly fight,
Lies the joy of winter's light.

Frost and Feathered Dreams

Cardinals rest on frosty limbs,
While penguins waddle in soft hymns,
The world drapes in silver's glow,
With every twinkle, off we go.

Snowy blankets hide the grass,
As hidden faces watch us pass,
Decked in winter's playful cheer,
We're wrapped in laughter, warm, sincere.

Mittens lost and scarves awry,
We laugh as snowflakes fill the sky,
With frosty noses, cheeks aglow,
Each step a clumsy, foolish show.

Under stars that shimmer bright,
We'll sip hot cocoa, pure delight,
In frost and dreams, let's dance along,
For winter's funny is our song.

Tones of the Wintery Whirl

Skiing down the frosty slope,
I hit a bump and lost my hope.
The snowflakes laugh, they shimmy 'round,
As I tumble down without a sound.

A squirrel dances on my hat,
Challenging me to a merry spat.
With each slip and icy grin,
Winter's humor makes me spin.

Frosty Fantasies on Snow-Blanketed Hills

Snowmen gather, having a ball,
With carrot noses, they stand tall.
One wears shades, another a tie,
They toast to snowstorms passing by.

The hills echo with giggles bright,
As snowballs fly in frosty fights.
A dog slides past with utmost glee,
While I trip over my own two feet.

Ember Light in Winter's Grasp

By the fire, hot cocoa in hand,
I spill it all like a clumsy band.
Marshmallows float like soft, fluffy boats,
While I ponder how to roast my coats.

The cat's found warmth, and so has the rug,
Chasing its tail, it gives me a shrug.
"Do you see this winter chaos here?"
I chuckle, embracing the chilly cheer.

Frigid Cadence of the Silent Woods

Woods whisper secrets in frosty air,
I try to listen, but I can't quite dare.
The trees warble tunes, a wintery choir,
While I stumble over a mischievous wire.

A raccoon appears, looking quite wise,
With snow on his nose and mischief in his eyes.
He seems to wink, as if to say,
"Winter's a stage, come join the play!"

Unraveled Secrets in Snowdrifts

Snowflakes tumble, light as air,
The squirrels dance without a care.
Winter wears a cozy frown,
While penguins slip around the town.

Giant snowmen with carrot noses,
Joke about the frozen roses.
They freeze their hats upon their heads,
And revel in their chilly beds.

Kids with mittens, laughs abound,
Slip on ice, then twirl around.
Hot cocoa spills on snowy clothes,
As frosty wind occasionally blows.

From rooftops, snowballs take flight,
An icy battle in the night.
Winter's laugh contains a twist,
A snowy fun, we can't resist.

Symphony of the Winter Sky

The clouds whistle their icy tune,
While carolers hum beneath the moon.
Snowflakes dance to a glacial beat,
As deer prance on their frosty feet.

Snowmen gossip with frosty cheer,
Telling tales of winter's year.
Their carrot lips can't stop the giggles,
While trees sway and do the wiggles.

Icicles clink like giant chimes,
In shadows made by frosted pines.
A winter breeze, a ticklish tease,
Whispers secrets among the trees.

Under stars, the night feels bright,
While snowflakes pirouette in flight.
Laughter echoes in the cold,
A winter symphony to behold.

Poems Wrapped in Frost

Frosty whispers creep at dawn,
A fluffy cat prances on the lawn.
Snowflakes tickle, a light-hearted brawl,
As winter's blanket covers all.

Thumbs up! A snowball goes astray,
Landing right on Grandma's way.
She chuckles while her glasses freeze,
To join the warm laughs carried by the breeze.

A hare hops by with a puffy scarf,
Chasing shadows, oh what a laugh!
Chasing tracks, they prance and play,
On a cheerful, snowy day.

Beneath the moon, laughter ignites,
While children bubble with joyful bites.
The world is bright, wrapped in frosty cheer,
A whimsical winter, come sit here!

Glacial Melodies of Solitude

In a quiet glade, the snowflakes hum,
Frosty giggles seem to come.
Lonely trees sway to the beat,
While winter friends play beneath their feet.

A bear slips up, it's quite a sight,
Tumbling softly in sheer delight.
His laugh echoes through the snowy lane,
As he finds joy in winter's reign.

Wind chimes tinkle, a gentle call,
While snowflakes lace the world in fall.
Snowy whispers float up high,
A frosty tune beneath the sky.

Ice skates clash, a clumsy glide,
As laughter and winter both coincide.
In chilly air, let dreams take flight,
For winter's magic feels just right.

Glacial Harmonies

Frosty feet dance on the ground,
Chilly giggles all around.
Snowflakes swirl like silly hats,
Winter laughs, oh how it chats.

Icicles hang, a frozen frown,
Teeth are chattering in the town.
Hot cocoa sips, as blush takes flight,
Socks that vanish in the night.

Snowmen wear a goofy grin,
With buttons lost, they still fit in.
Penguins slide, oh what a sight,
Creating laughter, pure delight.

Carrots tipped like crooked noses,
Winter's fun is full of poses.
Slip and slide, we all are brave,
In this chill, we misbehave.

Whispered Threads of Frost

Winter whispers, chilly breath,
Melting snowflakes tease our steps.
Scarves that tangle, hats askew,
Each frosty gust says, 'Look at you!'

Noses red, like cherries bright,
Brushing off the frosty bite.
Snowballs flying, giggles loud,
Mischief wraps us like a shroud.

Slippery slopes and snowy banks,
Laughter echoed, full of pranks.
Frosty fingers, hot tea neat,
Oh what joy 'neath winter's sheet!

Chasing snowflakes, one by one,
In winter's game, oh what fun!
We'll frolic until nightfall calls,
The frost will dance, the laughter sprawls.

Notes from a Shivering Dawn

Morning frost, a ticklish chill,
Sunrise sneezes, what a thrill!
Coffee warms our frozen hands,
As snowflakes land in funny bands.

Socks mismatched, a playful sight,
Hiccup squeaks from sheer delight.
Birds are puffed, their chirps a song,
In this season, we all belong.

Snowmen wobble with silly waves,
As winter's humor gently saves.
Toasting marshmallows by the fire,
Who knew cold could inspire?

Dawn breaks with laughter in its glow,
Ice skaters fall, but still they flow.
In this crisp air, we find a cheer,
Winter jesters bring us near.

Reflections of the Bitter Breeze

An icy breeze with a playful kick,
Snowflakes prance, they dance, they tick.
Furrowed brows but spirits high,
We wave at clouds that wander by.

Bitter winds bring laughter's fight,
Chasing sleds brings sheer delight.
With every slip, a cheer erupts,
Winter's chaos is what corrupts.

Chattering teeth sing out a tune,
While snowballs tumble, quite a boon.
Gloves enchanted with secrets spun,
In this chill, we all have fun.

Frosted twig and snowman's stake,
Giggles linger for goodness sake.
This brisk spell can't dampen the sass,
Funny moments always amass.

Ponderings Under the Winter Moon

Why does snow look like a big marshmallow?
The cold turns cheeks to a bright red halo.
Sledding down hills with wild, loud screams,
While hot cocoa dances in our dreams.

Frosty breath that looks like smoke,
Joking with snowmen, oh what a bloke!
Sneaking snowballs, a playful attack,
With laughter ringing, we'll never look back.

Ice skates wobble, we're all quite silly,
A slip on the ice, oh isn't that frilly?
With mittens bundled, hands tucked in tight,
We giggle and chortle till fall turns to night.

Under moonlight's glow, we stomp and prance,
In a wintery waltz, we take our chance.
With twinkling stars and a frosty spin,
We laugh at the chill, let the fun begin!

Harmonics of the Shivering Frost

Chattering teeth sing a chilly tune,
Dance with snowflakes under the moon.
Hot chocolate spills, oh what a mess,
Wrapped like burritos, it's winter's dress.

Icicles hang like wonky fangs,
As penguins pirouette in silly tangs.
The snowman's carrot nose is so stout,
We question if he's got a pout.

Snowball fights erupt, a laughing crowd,
Cheers and shrieks, we shout oh so loud!
Hands in pockets, we plot and scheme,
While winter wraps us in its cool dream.

With rosy noses and cheeks aglow,
Big fluffy hats make the fashion show.
The frigid air is filled with cheer,
As winter's quirks bring us near.

Chorus of the Icebound Heart

The cold wind whistles a quirky tease,
Frosty fingers tug at my sleeves.
Snowflakes twirl like ballerinas prance,
While squirrels debate on a nutty dance.

In thick parkas, we waddle around,
Making snow angels without a sound.
Giggles erupt with every slip,
As winter insists, it's a slippery trip.

Slippery sidewalks become our slide,
With laughter echoing, we take a ride.
The world outside dressed in white and bright,
Ignites our hearts with a silly delight.

Underneath the stars so bright and clear,
Carrot noses bring holiday cheer.
With rosy cheeks, we embrace the art,
Of humor wrapped in winter's heart.

Whims of Winter's Song

Waking up to a world of fluff,
Snow drifts call, isn't it tough?
The dog jumps high, makes a big splash,
While we stumble, trying not to crash.

Snowflakes fall like a cozy hug,
But every cold gust gives a shrug.
With mittens lost in the fluffy pile,
We laugh at the wintery, whimsical style.

Frosty noses, jolly cheers,
Merry-making with friends through the years.
Hot soup spills, a bubbly delight,
In the chill of the day, we'll take flight.

So here's to the frosty, funny times,
With twinkling stars and chimes of rhymes.
In the midst of snow and silliness grand,
We'll revel and dance, hand in hand!

Balmy Echoes Beneath the Ice

Ice cubes skate in winter's breeze,
A penguin slips with charm and ease.
Snowmen dance with carrot noses,
As snowflakes fall, the chaos growses.

Sleds turn into flying boats,
With laughter ringing, oh what hoat!
Chasing frost from cheek to cheek,
Winter's naughtiness at its peak.

Hot cocoa spills, a marshmallow fight,
Bonfires crackle, oh what a sight!
With mittens lost and scarves misplaced,
We trip on snow, but still embrace.

Beneath the chill, we twirl and spin,
What joy it is to play and grin.
Winter's wonder, a playful tease,
With silly fumbles that never freeze.

Cracked Laughter in the Snow

The frost is biting, but who cares?
We're snug in jackets, sans the layers.
Snowballs fly like meteorite,
But laughter echoes through the night.

Icicles dangle like silly hats,
While squirrels frolic, chasing cats.
Making snow angels, all aglow,
With jolly antics in icy show.

Nursery rhymes in the bitter chill,
Jingle bells ring, it's a snowy thrill.
Bundled tight, we scamper 'round,
Like snowflakes tumbling to the ground.

Crackling fires and cookies baked,
Our winter jest, we've truly raked.
The fun we find in frosty air,
Is cracked laughter everywhere!

Diaries of Frozen Whispers

The snowflakes tell their silly tales,
Of winter nights and snowman pales.
Whispers carry on the breeze,
As penguins waddle with such ease.

Their frosty steps leave prints so wide,
Their joyful giggles we cannot hide.
Frosted tips on noses bright,
We share our secrets in moonlight.

Wit and whimsy, oh what a pair,
With snowball fights and frosty air.
Underneath the glittering skies,
We pen our joys through laughing sighs.

In frozen diaries, stories thrive,
Each giggle nurtures joy alive.
In winter's hush, we find our cheer,
Through playful whispers, loud and clear.

Wistful Echoes of the Chill

A frosty breeze tickles our cheeks,
As winter pranks become our peaks.
With snowflakes swirling in the air,
We tumble down without a care.

Sipping cider in mittens bright,
Chatting 'bout our snowy plight.
Eager flakes waltz from the skies,
As giggles trumpet winter's lies.

The chilly fog plays peek-a-boo,
While snowmen tell jokes, yes it's true!
We jump and laugh, the world feels new,
Embracing mischief in the blue.

Winter echoes, a playful thrill,
In our hearts, it will fulfill.
Childlike wonder in every chill,
As whispers twinkle, moments still.

Memories in the Winter's Embrace

The snowflakes dance upon my nose,
And I can't quite tell which way it blows.
Warmed by hot cocoa, I laugh and grin,
As snowmen whisper, 'Let the fun begin!'

Frosty pants and clumsy slips,
Friends in mittens sharing sips.
We toss snowballs like we're pros,
And tumble down in white white clothes.

We may freeze, but spirits wake,
Garlic bread's what we will bake!
Winter games, a goofy show,
Jumping in piles, yelling, 'Whoa!'

If winter's chill gives us a fright,
We wrap in blankets, holding tight.
Giggles echo, the hearth aglow,
In cozy corners, warmth we know.

Compositions of the Icy Night

Stars are twinkling through the frost,
While snowmen sing, 'I'm not lost!'
Their carrot noses up in the air,
They serenade us—we stop and stare.

Chilly cheeks and frosted breath,
We dance around, flirting with death.
Slipping and sliding on ice that's slick,
Giggles erupt as we try a trick!

Snowflakes fall with a gentle sway,
Wrapping us up in winter's play.
The cold won't stop us from feeling free,
With snowball fights and hot tea spree!

We'll sing to the moon, oh so bright,
In hilarious hats, what a sight!
As the night drifts away from the glow,
We'll laugh at the frost, inviting the snow.

Chords of Timeless Serenity

In puffer coats, we stomp with flair,
To winter's tunes, we dance and share.
The chilly air filled with silly sounds,
Each note of laughter, our joy abounds.

Frozen pipes make showering tough,
But we just giggle, 'Oh, that's rough!'
Building forts, we rule the night,
With our puppy, all bundled tight.

Icicles hang like dangling glee,
Sipping hot soup is the key!
Snowflakes swirl, we twirl about,
With frosty breaths, we laugh and shout.

Moments freeze but spirits do not,
In this merry land, we'll give it a shot.
When winter calls, we'll bloom like flowers,
In the frosty air, we've got superpowers!

Flurries of Muffled Voices

We bundle up in woolly hats,
But can't find gloves—oh, the spats!
With snowflakes sticking to our cheeks,
We shout out silly winter tweaks.

The dog leaps in with boundless cheer,
As snowflakes kiss our laughing ear.
We forget complaints, just seek the fun,
In a wonderland, we all run!

Icicles drip like melted dreams,
We play the part, or so it seems.
Every step is a signature slip,
We laugh so hard, we might just flip!

Wrapping up in layered fluff,
Winter's antics are never tough.
With friends beside, we share the bliss,
In a world of snow, it's pure happiness!

Embrace of the Frosty Dawn

Oh, the ice capades of my morning cup,
Someone upsized my love for hot pup!
Birds in fluffy coats chirp cheerfully,
Wishing for muffins, not cold, that's me.

Snowflakes tango upon my nose,
Turning my pink toes into the froze.
Each breath a dragon's playful puff,
Winter's a joker, oh isn't it tough?

Crystalline Dreams of Winter Evenings

Under the chandelier of icy beams,
The cat's in a scarf, oh what a dream!
We dance with shadows, giving a wink,
Warming our toes with thoughts that we think.

Hot cocoa rivers flow through our hearts,
With marshmallow clouds, oh silly, it starts!
Our laughter's the best kind of winter cheer,
Chasing away all the grumpy and drear.

Harmonious Echoes of Stillness

The snowman's hat is a wintery crown,
He's got no arms, but don't let him frown.
We turn snowballs into silly fights,
While geese honk tunes under street lantern lights.

Nature's melody, a comedic score,
As squirrels wear socks and slide on the floor.
Echoes of joy fill the frosty air,
Who knew pure whimsy could come from a dare?

Twilight of the Shimmering Evergreens

As twilight hugs the pointy pine trees,
The wind whispers softly through chilly leaves.
A critter slips on a shimmering sheet,
A dance of pure laughter, how cute and sweet!

Pinecones tumble, making the squirrels laugh,
While I contemplate the snow angel's craft.
A holiday sweater that's two sizes wide,
In this fun frosty dance, we all take pride!

A Harmony for the Frozen Heart

Snowflakes drift, they tap dance down,
Silly hats worn by every town.
Hot cocoa flows, like rivers of cheer,
While penguins slide, let out a squeal.

Icicles hang like frozen spears,
Making snowmen drink their beers.
Frosty noses, cheeks so bright,
Chasing snowballs, what a sight!

Winter nights, with bonfires crack,
Marshmallows roast, no turning back.
Giggling pairs beneath the moon,
Dancing shadows to winter's tune.

Each frosty breath a cloud of giggles,
As snowflakes swirl, the laughter wiggles.
In the chill, friendships grow tight,
Winter wraps us in pure delight.

Fragments of a Winter's Identity

Squirrels clad in all their fuzz,
Chasing each other, making a buzz.
With snowball fights and goofy grins,
They tumble down with cheeky spins.

The deer in coats of fluffy white,
Look confused at the snowman's height.
They chuckle softly, share a glance,
Join in the drifts for a winter's dance.

Snowman parties, carrots in hand,
Gathered 'round the frosty land.
Don't forget a hat that's bright,
For a fashion show under stars so white.

Each flake a joke, a playful tease,
Landing softly, like winter's breeze.
In this chilly realm of the absurd,
Nature laughs, though rarely heard.

Whispers of Frosted Lullabies

The wind hums tunes, a chilly jest,
While snowflakes fall to take a rest.
Furry friends in cozy heaps,
Snoring sounds that silence creeps.

Glistening lights on trees they cling,
Mice breakdance to the jingle's ring.
Hot soup's brewing, a steamy show,
As winter's warmth sets hearts aglow.

A fluffy bunny hops with flair,
In a parade, with not a care.
They twirl and whirl, make snowmen smile,
Creating joy that warms a mile.

So sing along with frosty dreams,
As laughter flows in icy streams.
For in this season, we unite,
With chilly fun that feels just right.

Melodies Beneath the Ice

Under frozen skies, we skip and dash,
Ice skating now, a graceful splash.
With peppermint sticks, we change the game,
Untangling scarves, all the same.

Sleds whiz by, a humorous sight,
While snowmen argue who's built just right.
Twirling tales in the winter's glow,
As giggles echo 'neath the snow.

Mittens missing, toes get cold,
The winter's story, hilariously told.
We're wrapped in layers, like overstuffed pies,
Waddling home with prancing sighs.

With each plop and squish, let laughter reign,
Footprints left like a silly chain.
In winter's humor, we find our cheer,
Together, forever—warm to our feet here.

Frost-Kissed Reflections Under Stars

The snowman winks with a carrot nose,
He tells me jokes while the cold wind blows.
I trip on ice and then I laugh,
Snowflakes swirl like a silly photograph.

The stars above giggle, twinkling bright,
As I dance with shadows, a comical sight.
A reindeer chuckles from across the way,
I guess he's here for the holiday play.

Pine trees drip with glistening frost,
Each branch adorned, never a cost.
We slide and slide, like a clumsy crew,
In this frosty world, where laughter's the glue.

With frosty breath, we exclaim with glee,
Winter's a jest, come frolic with me!
Each laugh is bright, a joyous leap,
Under the stars, our secrets we keep.

Whirling Waltz of Snowy Elders

In the village square, old folks take a spin,
With rosy cheeks, and broad, toothy grins.
They twirl and twirl, like kids at play,
Who knew winter's chill could brighten the day?

Grandpa slips and does a little dance,
While Grandma laughs, taking a chance.
They share stories, proud, without a care,
Of snowstorms past and the frosty air.

Snowflakes fall like a playful shower,
As laughter grows with each snow-covered hour.
The elders cheer with every swirl,
In the heart of winter, their spirits unfurl.

With each turn they make, the snow gleams bright,
Their hearts are warm in the chilly night.
Together they whittle away their woes,
In this whirlwind of winter, where joy simply flows.

Overture of Glacial Moments

Icicles hang like chandeliers,
Glistening sharp, but they soothe our fears.
We slip-slide down with giggles and glee,
Even the dog joins our comedic spree.

Snowballs fly, a fluffy barrage,
Laughter erupts; it's a joyful mirage.
One hit the snooze button on a winter's nap,
A perfect wake-up, a hilarious clap!

We build a fort with leaves and snow,
Royalty! Kings and queens in a winter show.
But watch out, the roof might start to cave,
As laughter echoes, we dance like a rave.

Oh, glacial moments, freeze this delight,
In our frosty kingdom, mischief takes flight.
So raise a glass of cold, fizzy cheer,
To moments so silly in this time of year!

Sighs Beneath the Snowfall

Under blankets of white, we start to snooze,
But giggle monsters dance, won't let us choose.
The snow whispers secrets, can't catch a break,
As we cough up giggles for goodness' sake.

Snowflakes twirl down, tickling our cheeks,
Each one a jester that plays hide and seeks.
With every plop, another laugh's born,
Even the cat thinks it's frosty adorn.

A chill bites softly, yet spirits soar,
We'll laugh 'til we drop, never a bore.
The world gets blurry, afresh, looks like art,
Under snowfall's sighs, we'll never depart.

So here's to the frolic, the frosty delight,
Under falling snowflakes, we're all feeling light.
Let's cherish these moments, with laughs so free,
In our winter wonderland, just you and me.

Chords of the Winter Solstice

Snowflakes danced with glee,
While squirrels played a tune,
Their acorns rolled in sync,
A winter's funny boon.

Trees wore coats of white,
Like fashionistas bold,
Whispering frosty jokes,
While the wind laughed in cold.

Penguins slid with flair,
On ice like a grand stage,
While snowmen broke out laughs,
And danced without a cage.

Hot cocoa started a riot,
With marshmallows on top,
Each sip a silly giggle,
Till mugs just wouldn't stop.

Echoes of the Scarlet Sunset

The sun gave a wink,
As it dipped low and bright,
Clouds painted in laughter,
A comedic twilight.

Crimson skies crack jokes,
While the birds chirp along,
Each flutter and flap,
Like a whimsical song.

Trees gossip in hues,
With shadows that tease,
As dusk sprinkles humor,
On the evening's soft breeze.

Stars peek out in giggles,
From their blanket of night,
And the moon just chuckles,
In its silvery light.

Frosty Melodies in the Moonlight

The moon cracked a smile,
As snowflakes hit the ground,
Singing jokes to the stars,
With a frosty surround.

Rabbits wore cool shades,
As they hopped in a line,
Each jump a funny stunt,
Dancing through the pines.

Icicles shook with laughter,
While they hung from the eaves,
Each drop a tiny giggle,
As the winter wind weaves.

And snowballs tossed with flair,
In a frosty snowball fight,
Turned the night into laughter,
Under the moon's soft light.

The Stillness of Silvered Silence

In the stillness of night,
The world paused for a prank,
Silent whispers erupted,
From each frosted bank.

Snowmen plotted mischief,
With carrots for their plans,
While trees held their branches,
Like excited little fans.

The crisp air held its breath,
Waiting for a good jest,
As shadows played tag,
In this wintery quest.

And beneath all the stillness,
A giggle softly rang,
In the silvered silence,
Where the laughter sprang.

Lullabies in a Crystal Landscape

In a world where snowflakes dance,
Even penguins try to prance.
The rabbits wear their hats so snug,
While squirrels plot a snowball tug.

Trees giggle in their frosty coats,
As ducks parade on icy moats.
A snowman holds a carrot nose,
While cats tiptoe on frozen toes.

Bunnies sing their winter tunes,
While foxes chase the glowing moons.
Air balloons drift by with cheer,
As winter giggles, oh so near.

So come and join the snowy fun,
With every frosty, sparkling run.
We'll laugh and play till day is done,
In this landscape, winter's pun!

Harmonies of the Frosty Air

In chilly winds, the penguins waddle,
As they navigate the icy paddle.
Snowflakes swirl like confetti dreams,
Laughing softly in the moonbeams.

Polar bears in fuzzy hats,
Swinging sticks like chatty bats.
The penguin choir starts to croak,
To the beat of a frosty joke.

A reindeer dances on a spree,
Twisting round a frosty tree.
With laughter echoing so clear,
Winter's fun is always near.

So wrap yourself in muffled cheer,
With plump snowflakes, never fear.
In this frosty air, we'll play,
And share a chuckle every day!

Serenade of the Silent Pines

The pines whisper with icy breath,
As squirrels plot and plot for their heft.
Giggling softly in the glade,
Beneath the snowy, glorious shade.

With hoots and howls, the owls arrive,
In their winter cloaks, they come alive.
The bunnies bounce without a care,
Chasing shadows everywhere.

A snowball flies, oh what a sight,
As giggles echo through the night.
A prancing moose takes a silly fall,
And laughter blankets over all.

In the stillness, they all unite,
Under starry skies so bright.
With playful tunes and wintry signs,
We sing along with silent pines!

Ballad of the Shimmering Moonlight

Under a moon that shines and beams,
Bunnies glide on icy streams.
They giggle and slide all around,
While snowflakes twirl without a sound.

A fox attempts a forced moonwalk,
Stumbles over while trying to gawk.
The stars reply with twinkling laughter,
As winter's charm spins happily after.

The owls hoot with silly flair,
Chasing shadows everywhere.
With frosty breath and hearty cheer,
We gather close, our friends so near.

So let the winter chase your woes,
With sparkling laughs as cold wind blows.
We'll dance under moonlight's glow,
Where joy and giggles freely flow!

Serenade of Shimmering Snowflakes

Snowflakes tumble, oh so spry,
Falling down from painted sky.
Squirrels dance in winter coats,
While penguins try to take their notes.

Frosty friends with cheeks so round,
Hopping, slipping on the ground.
Hot cocoa makes a grand debut,
With marshmallows that wave 'how do you do?'

Icicles are the chandeliers,
Sparkling bright, bring out the cheers.
Snowman rolls, a jolly sight,
With a carrot nose, a sheer delight!

Laughter echoes, joyful sounds,
Winter fun in all surrounds.
Grab your sled, it's time to play,
A frosty feast, hip-hip-hooray!

Chants of the Crisp Twilight

Twilight settles, shadows dance,
Snowflakes twirl, it's time to prance.
Penguins slide on frozen lakes,
Making jokes to catch some flakes.

Crisp air tickles noses bright,
As polar bears get ready for flight.
They wear a scarf from head to toe,
In style, oh! They steal the show.

Hot chocolate dreams in mugs so wide,
As snowflakes join the winter ride.
Frolicking birds, with beaks so sweet,
Pecking crumbs from our cozy seat.

Bouncing bunnies make a fuss,
Tumbling through a snowy hush.
With every stomp and every hop,
Our laughter makes the moments pop!

Echoes Amidst the Winter's Veil

Winter whispers, a cheeky breeze,
Tickling quiet, dancing trees.
Bells are jingling, pets all prance,
While fluffballs join the waltzing dance.

Frosty noses, cheeks aglow,
Falling down with quite a show.
A snowball fight, oh what a sight,
Laughter reigns till the moon is bright.

Mittens lost in a snowy heap,
While dreaming of candy, ice-cream steep.
Sleds collide with the greatest ease,
As winter hums, "It's all a tease!"

Footprints lead to adventure bright,
In the glow of silver light.
Join the waltz and let it flow,
Embrace the cheer as cold winds blow!

Harmonies on a Frozen Breath

Chilly whispers ride the night,
Creating sparkles, pure delight.
Laughter bounces, fills the air,
As frosty friends bring joy and flair.

Wobbling snowmen, give a smile,
With hats so grand, they flaunt their style.
Skiing squirrels zip all around,
While snowflakes play on icy ground.

Breezy tunes of winter's jest,
Bringing warmth to every quest.
With cocoa cheers, we take a sip,
As giggles fly, we laugh and flip.

Glistening nights, oh what a thrill,
Under stars, our spirits fill.
In cozy blankets, we all nest,
Winter's charm, it is the best!

Milton Keynes UK
Ingram Content Group UK Ltd.
UKHW021241191124
451300UK00007B/175